# Foreclosure Investing with Homes for Sale in NY

## How to Find, Finance & Market Foreclosures in NY

# Neilson Roberts

# TABLE OF CONTENTS

# DEDICATION

**This book is dedicated to my son's**
**Christian and Matthew.**
**A blessing from God and the joy of my life.**

## ACKNOWLEDGMENTS

I WOULD LIKE TO ACKNOWLEDGE ALL THE HARD WORK OF THE MEN AND WOMEN OF THE UNITED STATES MILITARY, WHO RISK THEIR LIVES ON A DAILY BASIS, TO MAKE THE WORLD A SAFER PLACE.

# Disclaimer

This book was written as a guide to starting a business. As with any other high yielding action, starting a business has a certain degree of risk. This book is not meant to take the place of accounting, legal, financial or other professional advice. If advice is needed in any of these fields, you are advised to seek the services of a professional.

While the author has attempted to make the information in this book as accurate as possible, no guarantee is given as to the accuracy or currency of any individual item. Laws and procedures related to business are constantly changing.

Therefore, in no event shall Brian Mahoney or MahoneyProducts Publishers be liable for any special, indirect, or consequential damages or any damages whatsoever in connection with the use of the information herein provided.

# Chapter 1

# Foreclosure Overview

# Foreclosure Overview

## What is Foreclosure

A foreclosure is when a bank, or the mortgage holder of a property takes the property of a homeowner who has not made interest and/or principal payments on time as stipulated in the mortgage contract.

## Types of Foreclosure

### Judicial Foreclosure

A house sold by judicial foreclosure is a mortgaged property sold by the courts. The bank or owner of the property get the proceeds, then other lien holders and even the borrower if there is anything left after the sale. Judicial foreclosures take place in all 50 states and U.S. territories.

The lender begins the process of a judicial foreclosure by filing a lawsuit against the borrower. Since it is a legal action, everyone involved must be notified of the proceedings. Notification of the proceedings can vary from state to state(classified ads to posted notices). There is usually a hearing to determine the proceedings.

# Foreclosure Overview

## Nonjudicial Foreclosure

Some jurisdictions allow lenders to foreclose property without getting a court order first (power of sale clause). This is called a non-judicial foreclosure.

Non-judicial foreclosure is only available for deeds of trust with power-of-sale clauses. They are not available for traditional mortgages.

Where available, non-judicial foreclosures are heavily regulated. Generally, before foreclosing, lenders must give special notice to the property-owner. Afterwards, lenders must wait a specified time before auctioning off the property.

## Strict Foreclosures

Strict foreclosure is only available in a few states like Connecticut, New Hampshire and Vermont. If a mortgagee wins a court case, the court orders the defaulted mortgagor to pay the mortgage within a specified period of time. Should the mortgagor fail to do so, the mortgage holder gains the title to the property with no obligation to sell it. This type of foreclosure is generally available only when the value of the property is less than the debt.

# Foreclosure Overview

## Real Estate Investor

Start-up Cost:                    $10,000 - $50,000

Potential Earnings:               $25,000 - Unlimited

Typical Fees:                     No money down to unlimited

Advertising:                      Real Estate Publications. Real Estate Agents. Social media.

Qualifications:                   Knowledge of the real estate market. Access to Capital. Maintenance Knowledge.

Equipment Needed:                 Cell phone. Computer. Internet access.  Home repair tools.

# Foreclosure Overview

Home Business Potential:    Yes

Staff Required:    Yes & No.

Hidden Cost:    Appraisals, interest, finance fees, eviction costs, downturns in the real estate market.

## Start up costs

Recently I purchased a 5 bedroom home with over half an acre back yard for under $7,000 from a bank. So you can litterally start your business with 1 or 2 credit cards if you have no money at all.

Later in this book you will be shown how to find real estate at a deep discount on a consistant basis. Many people simply don't believe they can purchase property for the price of a automobile. They have been culturally programmed to start out with an apartment, then go to a real estate agent to purchase a home. That is one reason there are so many low cost homes available. A recession and the economy in general is another. What ever the reason, great deals are almost everywhere.

# Foreclosure Overview

## Potential Earnings

I have made tens of thousands of dollars flipping property and rented property out for hundreds of dollars of monthly positive cash flow. Both have their advantages. Either way your potential earnings are limitless. The most important thing is to understand total cost.

Total Cost is the total amount of money expended to establish an investment position. Total cost includes commissions, accrued interest, and taxes, in addition to the principal amount of securities traded. Anticipate all costs, **<u>before</u>** you invest in a property.

## Advertising

Real estate magazines and online classified ads(craigslist) are a great place to advertise a home for sale or rent. However, Social Media has become more and more relevant in the real estate investing business. There are all types of social media web sites. Pinterest, Facebook, Instagram and Twitter to name a fee. However for real estate investing I believe there is no substitute for YouTube. From the comfort of their home, a person can take a complete walk through your property. YouTube is free and reatively easy to get started. A complete YouTube tutorial is included in this book.

# Foreclosure Overview

## Qualifications: Knowledge of the Market

A man's machine broke. He spent hours, then days trying to fix it. Finally he called a professional repair man. In just a few seconds, the repair man pulled out a hammer, whacked the machine and it was fixed. The man was handed a bill of $100. The man said "I'm not paying you $100 for just swinging your hammer." The repair man responded "you are not paying a $100 to me for swinging my hammer. You are paying a $100 to me for knowing where and how to swing my hammer."

Success in real estate investing is not complicated. Buy low. Sell higher. You simply need to know, what is low and how to find it. There is no substitute for patience and research. When I purchased that home from the bank for $7,000, I had been going online for 3 hours a day for months, viewing properties from multiple real estate web sites.

Viewing so many homes, gave me a masterful knowledge of the market, so I could then easily determine what is low and what is high in the market. It also gave me an idea of how long it took for properties to sell and for how much. Every market is different. Don't take real estate agent's word for things. Make their word part of determining the market for yourself.

# Foreclosure Overview

## Equipment Needed

Today you need a cell phone, a computer and a good internet connection to be an effective real estate investor. When you are starting out, it may also help if you have an ability to do some property repairs yourself.

Places like Home Depot and Lowes offer free classes on many typical home repairs. If you are going to do repairs yourself, then you will also need to add home repair tools, like circular saw, hammer, wrenches and drills, to the list of "equipment needed".

## Staff Required

Do you need a staff? Yes and no. No, because you don't have to have people on payroll. Yes because you are going to need assistance to run this business effectively.

Your team should include but not be limited to, a real estate attorney, several quality real estate agents, at least 2 handymen, and a bank loan officer or private money lender.

# Foreclosure Overview

## Hidden Costs

Attorney fees, Appraisals, interest, finance fees, eviction costs, downturns in the real estate market. Are just a few of the hidden costs in real estate investing.

When hiring an attorney, make sure you find one that specializes in real estate investing. One who knows contracts inside and out. Making this quality investment will help to reduce the cost on the majority of the other hidden fees.

# Chapter 2

# Finding Real Estate in New York

Quick & Easy Access to Foreclosure Real Estate

# Getting Started

When Investing in New York first you have to determine what county you want to purchase in. To help you decide, below is a list of all counties in New York with their population and square miles. After the list of all the counties, you get a Goldmine Rolodex of web site address of Wholesale Government Tax Sale Properties and More!

## New York Counties  Population  Sq Miles

| New York Counties | Population | Sq Miles |
|---|---|---|
| Kings County | 2,504,700 | 96.9 |
| Queens County | 2,230,722 | 178.28 |
| New York County | 1,585,873 | 33.77 |
| Suffolk County | 1,493,350 | 2,373 |
| Bronx County | 1,385,108 | 57.43 |
| Nassau County | 1,339,532 | 453 |
| Westchester County | 949,113 | 500 |
| Erie County | 919,040 | 1,227 |
| Monroe County | 744,344 | 1,366 |
| Richmond County | 468,730 | 102.5 |
| Onondaga County | 467,026 | 806 |

# New York Counties  Population  Sq Miles

| County | Population | Sq Miles |
|---|---|---|
| Orange County | 372,813 | 839 |
| Rockland County | 311,687 | 199 |
| Albany County | 304,204 | 533 |
| Dutchess County | 297,488 | 825 |
| Oneida County | 234,878 | 1,213 |
| Saratoga County | 219,607 | 844 |
| Niagara County | 216,469 | 1,140 |
| Broome County | 200,600 | 715 |
| Ulster County | 182,493 | 1,161 |
| Rensselaer County | 159,429 | 665 |
| Schenectady County | 154,727 | 210 |
| Chautauqua County | 134,905 | 1,500 |
| Oswego County | 122,109 | 1,312 |
| Jefferson County | 116,229 | 1,857 |
| St. Lawrence County | 111,944 | 2,821 |
| Ontario County | 107,931 | 662 |
| Tompkins County | 101,564 | 476 |

# New York Counties   Population   Sq Miles

| | Population | Sq Miles |
|---|---|---|
| Putnam County | 99,710 | 246 |
| Steuben County | 98,990 | 1,404 |
| Wayne County | 93,772 | 1,384 |
| Chemung County | 88,830 | 410.81 |
| Clinton County | 82,128 | 1,118 |
| Cattaraugus County | 80,317 | 1,310 |
| Cayuga County | 80,026 | 864 |
| Sullivan County | 77,547 | 997 |
| Madison County | 73,442 | 662 |
| Warren County | 65,707 | 870 |
| Livingston County | 65,393 | 640 |
| Herkimer County | 64,519 | 1,458 |
| Washington County | 63,216 | 846 |
| Columbia County | 63,096 | 648 |
| Otsego County | 62,259 | 1,003 |
| Genesee County | 60,079 | 495 |
| Fulton County | 55,531 | 533 |

# New York Counties  Population  Sq Miles

| New York Counties | Population | Sq Miles |
|---|---|---|
| Franklin County | 51,599 | 1,697 |
| Tioga County | 51,125 | 523 |
| Chenango County | 50,477 | 898.85 |
| Montgomery County | 50,219 | 410 |
| Cortland County | 49,336 | 502 |
| Greene County | 49,221 | 658 |
| Allegany County | 48,946 | 1,034 |
| Delaware County | 47,980 | 1,468 |
| Orleans County | 42,883 | 817 |
| Wyoming County | 42,155 | 596 |
| Essex County | 39,370 | 1,916 |
| Seneca County | 35,251 | 325 |
| Schoharie County | 32,749 | 626 |
| Lewis County | 27,087 | 1,290 |
| Yates County | 25,348 | 376 |
| Schuyler County | 18,343 | 342 |
| Hamilton County | 4,836 | 1,808 |

# New York

As of the writting of this book, all of these websites are up and running. From time to time some will change their address. If a site does not come up sometimes using the root of the address works. For example if www.mystate.gov/wholesaleproperty does not work. Just go with www.mystate.gov/

## New York Tax Sale/Foreclosure PROPERTIES

### New York City

http://www1.nyc.gov/site/finance/taxes/property-lien-sales.page

### Allegany county

http://www.alleganyco.com/tax-sale/

### Nassau County

https://www.nassaucountyny.gov/527/Annual-Tax-Sale-Lien

# Locate Statewide New York Properties

## MLS

http://www.mls.com/search/new-york.mvc

New York Real Estate Foreclosures with links to different cities on the landing page.

## REALTOR

http://www.realtor.com/realestateandhomes-search/New%20York

Links to New York real estate properties by county and city.

# UNITED STATES REAL ESTATE INFO

http://www.statelocalgov.net/50states-tax-authorities.cfm

http://www.brbpub.com/free-public-records/

www.RealAuction.com

www.GrantStreet.com

# Locate Nationwide Foreclosure Auction Properties

**http://www.bid4assets.com/**

Bid4assets is an amazing website for quickly finding investment property. The landing page has a map of the United States and you can just move your mouse pointer over the state you are interested in to see if they have any property in their database.

Here are just a few of assets you can target on this site!

* County Tax Sales

* Bank Owned Property

* US Marshal

* Real Estate

* Coins

* $1 No Reserve Homes

# Locate Nationwide Foreclosure Auction Properties

Http://www.realauction.com

Real Auction is another great website for instant access to property information.

Once on the landing page click "client sites".

They have 4 categories of information.

* Tax Liens Auctions

* Tax Deeds Applications

* Foreclosure and Tax Deed Auctions

* Tax Deed Management

Then chose from the states and counties that appear, that they have auction information.

# Nationwide Banks & Foreclosure Properties

## Bank of America

http://foreclosures.bankofamerica.com/

## Wells Fargo

https://reo.wellsfargo.com/

## Ocwen Financial Corporation

http://www.ocwen.com/reo

## Hubzu

http://www.hubzu.com/

# Government Foreclosure Properties

## Fannie Mae
## The Federal National Mortgage Association

https://www.fanniemae.com/singlefamily/reo-vendors

# CHAPTER 3

# Finding Wholesale Investment Property

**How to Find Wholesale Residential & Commercial Real Estate**

# How To Find Wholesale Real Estate

There are several basic methods to find real estate at wholesale prices. There are foreclosures and pre-foreclosures, so get excited! There are hundreds of great deals just waiting for you to find them! The first method is Searching Public Records.

## Searching Public Records

Go to your county's recorders office and look for notice of default or notice of sale. The advantage of this method is that many newly posted properties have not been seen by your competition. The disadvantage is that it usually takes more time to find property than the other methods.

Here is a tip. When ever a county clerk helps you, get that person's name and thank them face to face. Then go home and call the office and thank them again. Wait about a week. Then purchase a thank you card and mail it. Your kindness is going to stand out to that clerk. In turn that clerk is not likely to forget you.  You in turn will likely have an ally in that office. The old saying "It's not what you know, but who you know." This method helps the clerk and yourself get to know each other quicker than usual. At the very least, you should feel good for being a nice person!

# How To Find Wholesale Real Estate

Another advantage to searching public records is Probate Properties. You will need to be educated in your local area's probate laws to purchase those properties.

Probate is required for all estates that are not protected by a trust. The average duration of probate is 7 to 8 months.

If the house is owned outright, the estate is responsible for remitting property taxes and insurance premiums throughout the probate process.

Estate administrators can elect to sell the property if it is causing financial harm to the estate. If the estate does not have sufficient funds to cover outstanding debts, the probate judge can order the property sold.

How a probate house is sold depends on the type of probate that is used. "Court Confirmation" is the most common type of probate used. A judge must approve all of the aspects of the management of the estate. Independent Administration of Estate's Act (IAEA) governs the 2$^{nd}$ type of probate administration. It allows estate executors to engage in estate administrative affairs without the court management.

# How To Find Wholesale Real Estate

To purchase probate property you have to know which probate system is being applied. Properties can be bought directly from the estate executor when Independent Administration of Estate's process is in effect. You can place your bid through the court system when court approval is required.

An investor interested in finding probate real estate must research public records. When people pass away their last will and testament is recorded in the probate court. The last will and testament will contain valuable information such as the estate assets, who is the beneficiary, and contact info for whoever is administrating for the estate.

Property records should show if there are any liens on the property and if so, who holds the lien. They should also show the properties appraised value, the year it was constructed, the square footage and the lot size. The records may also help you to determine if there have been any tax liens placed on the property.

Do your due diligence when purchasing any type of real estate. Bring in professional help in the form of building inspectors, lawyers and any other professionals that can help protect you when needed.

# How To Find Wholesale Real Estate

## Using the Internet

I will provide you with a Small Real Estate Rolodex of web sites later in this chapter. Many are completely free and have tons of information. One success algorithm for buying a property is that you should never, never, purchase one property without looking at, at least 100 other properties. Being able to search online makes using this formula very easy.

## Using Local Papers and Journals

Local papers and journals. By law many foreclosures have to be posted in the local paper. This can mean a goldmine of opportunity for you. With newspaper circulation in decline, many people are simply not looking in the newspaper anymore. Advantage you.

Next I am going to cover several categories of real estate sources.

**\* Nationwide banks & Foreclosure Properties**

**\* Government Foreclosure Properties**

**\* Commercial Real Estate**

**\* FSBO  - For Sale By Owner**

# How To Find Wholesale Real Estate

## Nationwide Banks & Foreclosure Properties

### Bank of America

http://foreclosures.bankofamerica.com/

I have purchased property using this web site. It is my favorite because they have a large nationwide inventory and their web site is easy to navigate and sort properties.

### Wells Fargo

https://reo.wellsfargo.com/

Place yourself on their mailing list, and get property updates on a monthly basis.

### Ocwen Financial Corporation

http://www.ocwen.com/reo

Founded in 1988 they are one of the largest mortgage companies in America.

# How To Find Wholesale Real Estate

## Hubzu

http://www.hubzu.com/

Hubzu is a nationwide real estate auction web site. Very easy to use. This is a great web site for comparing property prices nationwide.

# How To Find Wholesale Real Estate

## Government Foreclosure Properties

One advantage purchasing from the government is that there is no emotional attachment to the property. Don't be afraid to make a offer that is lower than the listed price. I once argued with a real estate agent who refused to place a offer lower than the stated price. Eventually I got him to place the offer. (Remember that they work for you, however some government properties can't be purchased unless you go through a HUD or government approved agent.) It was countered twice, before I decided to purchase another property. But they countered with two offers lower than the listed price.

If you are reading a ebook version of this book then you should be able to access these web sites by clicking the links below. But if you are reading a paperback version of this book then be careful when looking for government properties. There are many web sites pretending to be government web sites and some will attempt to charge you fees for information about government properties.

# How To Find Wholesale Real Estate

# Government Foreclosure Properties

## Fannie Mae
## The Federal National Mortgage Association

https://www.fanniemae.com/singlefamily/reo-vendors

## Department of Housing and Urban Development

https://www.hudhomestore.com/Home/Index.aspx

## The Federal Deposit Insurance Corporation

https://www.fdic.gov/buying/owned/

## The United States Department of Agriculture

https://properties.sc.egov.usda.gov/resales/index.jsp

## United States Marshals

https://www.usmarshals.gov/assets/sales.htm#real_estate

# How To Find Wholesale Real Estate

# Commercial Real Estate Properties

## City Feet

is a nationwide database of Commercial Real Estate Property

http://www.cityfeet.com/#

## The Commercial Real Estate Listing Service

is a nationwide database of Commercial Real Estate Property

https://www.cimls.com/

## Land . Net

is a nationwide database of land, commercial real estate for sale and for lease.

http://www.land.net/

## Loop . Net

is a nationwide database of Commercial Real Estate Property

http://www.loopnet.com/

# How To Find Wholesale Real Estate

## FSBO – For Sale By Owner

### By Owner

http://www.byowner.com/

### For sale by owner in Canada

http://www.fsbo-bc.com/

### For sale by owner Central

http://www.fsbocentral.com/

### For sale by Owner: world's largest FSBO web site

http://www.forsalebyowner.com/

### Ranch by owner

http://www.ranchbyowner.com/

# Chapter 4

# Buy with no money down Colossal Cash CrowdFunding

# Crowd Funding Crowd Sourcing

In 2015 over $34 billion dollars was raised by crowdfunding. Crowdfunding and Crowdsourcing roots began in 2005 and they help to finance or fund projects by raising money from a large number of people, usually by using the internet.

This type of fundraising or venture capital usually has 3 components. The individual or organization with a project that needs funding, groups of people who donate to the project, and a organization sets up a structure or rules to put the two together.

These websites do charge fees. The standard fee for success is about %5. If your goal is not met there is also a fee.

Below is a list of the top Crowdfunding websites according to myself and Entrepreneur Magazine Contributor Sally Outlaw.

# Crowd Funding Crowd Sourcing

## https://www.indiegogo.com/

Started as a platform for getting movies made, now helps to raise funds for any cause.

## http://rockethub.com/

Started as a platform for the arts, now it helps to raise funds for business, science, social projects and education.

## http://peerbackers.com/

Peerbackers focuses on raising funds for business, entrepreneurs and innovators.

## https://www.kickstarter.com/

The most popular and well know n of all the crowdfunding websites. Kickstarter focuses on film, music, technology, gaming, design and the creative arts. Kickstarter only accepts projects from the United States, Canada and the United Kingdom.

# Crowd Funding Crowd Sourcing

## Group Growvc

### http://group.growvc.com/

This website is for business and technology innovation.

### https://microventures.com/

Get access to angel investors. This website is for business startups.

### https://angel.co/

Another website for business startups.

### https://circleup.com/

Circle up is for innovative consumer companies.

### https://www.patreon.com/

If you start a YouTube Channel (highly recommended) you will hear about this website frequently. This website is for creative content people.

# Crowd Funding Crowd Sourcing

## https://www.crowdrise.com/

"Raise money for any cause that inspires you."
The Landing page  slogan speaks for itself. #1
fundraising website for personal causes.

## https://www.gofundme.com/

This fundraising website allows for business,  charity,
education, emergencies, sports, medical, memorials,
animals, faith, family, newlyweds etc...

## https://www.youcaring.com/

The leader in free fundraising. Over $400 million
raised.

## https://fundrazr.com/

FundRazr is an award-winning online fundraising
platform  that has helped thousands of people and
organizations  raise money
for causes they care about.

# CHAPTER 5

# REAL ESTATE FINANCING 4,000 Sources!

## 8 Realistic Ways to Finance Real Estate

# FINANCING REAL ESTATE

**Welcome to Expert financing. I am going to show you several realistic ways to finance real estate. You are going to learn how to finance real estate with.**

* VA LOANS

* PARTNERS

* INVESTMENT CLUBS

* CREDIT CARDS

* CORPORATE CREDIT

* EQUITY

* SELLER FINANCE

* HARD MONEY LENDERS

* AND FINALLY I SHOW YOU THE MONEY$ !!

## USING A VA LOAN

According to the web sites www.benefits.va.gov and www.military.com the current VA Loan amount is a whopping $417,000! What a lot of veterans don't know is that you can use that money to purchase not only your home, but investment properties. That is how I started my investing career. Purchasing multiple homes using my VA Loan.

# FINANCING REAL ESTATE

Even if you are not a veteran, you can still partner up with one, who still has some money left on his or her VA LOAN.

If you are a Veteran, you will need to obtain a copy of your DD 214 and VA Form 26-1880 Request for a Certificate of Eligibility.

## PARTNERS

This is another way I purchased a home. At the time I worked for the United States Postal Service. I had already purchased plenty of homes, so many of the workers were aware I had successfully invested in real estate. At break time I went around and ask people to partner up with me. I had multiple people offer to go in as a partner. I choose one and that house we rehabbed and flipped just two months after purchasing it. To this day it was the biggest gross profit on one deal, I have had. True I had to split it with my partner, but I would rather have half of something than all of nothing.

Having the combined resources of two people can be a great benefit, but it is not without it's challenges. If you are going to use a partner, no matter how close you are...GET EVERY THING IN WRITING.

# FINANCING REAL ESTATE

Having a partner can dramatically increase the chance of a Bank lending money as well as having someone to split the work on rehabbing, should you decide to save money and make repairs yourself. But all this must be spelled out BEFORE you enter into a Agreement/Contract and purchase a home.

It helps if the person is like minded and understands the risks and benefits of investing, and truly understands the return on investment of a particular deal.

## REAL ESTATE INVESTMENT CLUBS

Real estate investment clubs are groups that meet locally and allow investors and other professionals to network and learn. They can provide extremely useful information for both the novice and expert real estate investor. A top real estate club can provide a great forum to network, learn about reputable contractors, brokers, realtors, lawyers, accountants and other professionals. On the other hand, there are many real estate clubs designed to sell you. They bring in "gurus" who sell either on stage or at the back of the room, and as a result, the clubs typically profit to the tune of %50 of the sale price of the product, bootcamp, or training that is pitched.

# FINANCING REAL ESTATE

I have purchased a ton of real estate books and real estate courses. Carlton Sheets, Dave Del Dotto, The Mylands, Seminar courses and much much more. I am not against any club bringing in a speaker who has a course. However I think there should be transparency to the members of the club.

There is certainly value in the networking that may come at one of these groups. But attend working to attain your goals and not necessarily the club's goal to sell you something. Some times both are the same thing. As a rule I usually leave debit cards at home the first time I attend an event. If there is a seller there with a "This day only offer" then I won't feel pressured to purchase. Plus most sellers can be convinced to sell at the discount offer price at a later time when you have had a chance to come down off the "sense of urgency emotional pitch" .

## CREDIT CARDS

When using a credit card in real estate you must really do your homework on the deal. Dan Kennedy a world famous marketer once said "always stack the numbers in your favor". That's how you use a credit card. Look at the return on investment as compared to the long term cost of using a credit card and it's interest. Also I would recommend buying low cost homes that you can purchase and own free and clear.

# FINANCING REAL ESTATE

No Mortgage Payment!!! My last 2 homes I have purchased have been cash deals. One home cost $1,500 and the other about $7,000. The first was a government property from HUD and the 2nd From a Bank. These institutions are unemotional about real estate and simply view a property as a non performing asset. The 2nd home was 4 bedrooms, 1 1/2 bath and a basement located in a farming community and came with a 2 car garage/shed and   .6 acre(that is the size of a NFL football field) of land.

In this book I show you how to find plenty of houses with amazing below wholesale prices and a formula for almost always finding a great deal.

## CORPORATE CREDIT

Many people set up corporations to buy and sell real estate as an additional protection against liabilities. Other's create a corporation to mask personal involvement in property transfers and public records. Regardless of the use of a corporation, you can buy real estate with corporate credit as an alternative to using your own cash or IRA. By capitalizing on the credit rating of your corporation, you can buy real estate and build your corporate holdings portfolio.

# FINANCING REAL ESTATE

Just remember that you can set up your corporation in a state that favors you the most for your real estate deals. Do your research. Most people like Delaware and Nevada, but you will have to decide if your home state or any other state is best for you and your business.

## CURRENT EQUITY

Using the equity in your home for real estate investing is another way you can finance properties. You might use the money for a down payment or it may only be enough to cover the cost of some rehab repairs.

If you stick to the low cost home formula, you may have enough to purchase the entire house.  A house is an investment that should appreciate in value as well as give a great ROI (Return On Investment). When you decide to flip the property or rent it out for positive cashflow.

If you have equity and it's not doing anything, then you may decide to make it a "performing asset" and use it as part of your real estate finance program.

# FINANCING REAL ESTATE

## SELLER FINANCING

Seller finance is where the seller of a free and clear property becomes your bank along with being the seller.

Advantages:

You get to purchase the property on terms that may be more beneficial for you.  Seller gets monthly payments and the benefit of treating the sale as an installment sale thus allowing them to defer any capital gains taxes that may be due.

Disadvantages:

You may be locked into a mortgage with a pre-payment penalty or may not be able to resell the property immediately.  This strategy is typically not meant for flipping but can definitely be used for that purpose if structured correctly.

Seller Finance is a known way to finance a property.  That is why I have presented it in this book.  But it is my least favorite because you now have a lingering relationship with your property.  Your ability to make decisions regarding the property is limited and for that reason, I would not go this route.  However, like all types of financing, you have to ask yourself, "is the deal worth it."

# FINANCING REAL ESTATE

I also prefer to work alone, but when a great deal came along, I sought out a partner to make it happen. Risk is usually relative to potential profit.

# HARD MONEY LENDERS

A hard money lender is usually a individual or company that lends money for an investment secured by the investment property.

Advantages:

Less red tape to get the money. You are dealing with people who understand the real estate investment business.

Disadvantage:

This is not a long term loan. The lender wants a return on investment, usually within a few months, a a year, or a few years.  The interest rate on the loan is much higher than usual conventional banks.

Using hard money has a higher risk because the return on investment is due quicker. Therefore it is a good idea not to use a Hard Money Lender, until you have a great deal of experience and confidence in being able to produce a return on investment.

# SHOWING YOU THE MONEY

## A list of web sites for financing.

www.businessfinance.com (4,000 sources of money!)

www.advanceamericaproperty.com

http://www.cashadvanceloan.com/

www.brookviewfinancial.com

www.commercialfundingcorp.com

www.dhlc.com
(hard money for the Texas area)

www.equity-funding.com

www.bankofamerica.com

www.carolinahardmoney.com
(for real estate investors in North and South Carolina)

## www.fpfloans.com

# FINANCING REAL ESTATE

As you can see there are plenty of strategies for financing a property. Do your research on your investment property and get the true market value. Purchase well below wholesale. This will help to minimize risk and elevate your potential profit margins. Buying below wholesale also creates a buffer for unexpected expenses.

So don't let the lack of money be a roadblock in your real estate investing dreams.

# Chapter 6
# Managing Your Rental Properties

# Managing Your Rental PROPERTIES

## Keeping the Property Clean

You should have your property always as clean as possible. Curbside appeal can attract new tenants and make the tenants you have, desire to stay.

Have maintanance personnel make a routine inspection of the property to make  sure that trash and debris are taken care of.

Larger properties may require a commercial property cleaning service.

Keep your property landscaped  and the grass at the proper length. Again this adds to the curb appeal.

Part of keeping your property clean is to have an extermination company keep your property free of unwanted pests, like rodents and roaches.

## Property Security

The property should be well lit. Light helps deter crime. However good lighting might not be enough. You may need to hire a security service to patrol the grounds or at least be on call, depending on the crime in the area.

Tenants may move out, if they don't feel safe. So make  your tenants feel protected. Having security on property can deter crime and give the tenants a better feeling of comfort.

# Managing Your Rental PROPERTIES

## Financial Management and Record Keeping

### Software

Recently property management software prices have lowered and that has increased it's popularity. Software technology is allowing property managers to save time and run a more efficent business. Below are some of the top property management software programs currently on the market. All information, copy and pricing was taken from their website.

## Property management software

### 123LandLord

### http://www.123landlord.com/

123Landlord allows you to manage all of your tenants and properties, collect payments and track rent due.

They Currently have 5 versions.

| | | | |
|---|---|---|---|
| Free | free | 2 tenants | 2 properties |
| Professional | $13 a month | 12 tenants | 12 properties |
| Premier | $29 a month | 50 tenants | 50 properties |
| Deluxe | $49 a month | 75 tenants | 75 properties |
| Enterprise | $79 a month | Unlimited | Unlimited |

# Managing Your Rental PROPERTIES

## Financial Management and Record Keeping

### Acturent

### Forms

Preloaded legal forms save you time and money.

### Website

Acturent allows you to build a custom website for your organization at no extra charge.

### Tenant Services

Advertise your availabilities online, accept online payments, online applications, and much more...

Offers service and support by email.

They charge a base fee of $5 a month plus .30 cents per unit.

**https://acturent.com/**

# Managing Your Rental PROPERTIES

## Financial Management and Record Keeping

### AppFolio

"AppFolio Property Manager is designed for property managers who want to automate, modernize, and grow their business. Whether you manage multifamily, single-family, student housing, HOA, condo, or commercial properties- or maybe you manage a mixed portfolio - our all-in-one cloud-based solution has features built specifically for you so you can streamline your workday and focus on your bottom line."

Residental $1.25  per unit a month

Commercial $1.50 per unit a month

Student Housing $1.25 per unit a month

Community Associations $.80 per unit a month

**http://www.appfolio.com/**

# Managing Your Rental PROPERTIES

There are plenty of property management companies, and with modern technology creating better management software, you have plenty of options for managing your rental property.

# Chapter 7
# YouTube
# Video
# Marketing

# YouTube Video Marketing
## Overview

Million Dollar Video Marketing

When you read the title of this book you may have thought the term "Million Dollar" was hyperbole. However the beauty of video marketing is that it can be done for free, and that there really are several people who make millions of dollars just on their YouTube video's alone. Meaning that they allow ads to be placed on them and they get paid a portion of what google gets from businesses that runs the ads.

Since they are only getting a portion of what is being paid, that means if they make a million dollars, the video's actually produced multi-millions of dollars in ad revenue.

Here are a list of YouTube Millionaires as reported by Forbes magazine in the 20 December 2016 issue.

| Youtube name/channel | 2016 Income |
|---|---|
| 1. Pewdiepie | $15 Million |

Makes video's of himself playing video games and making crude comments on girls dancing.

| | |
|---|---|
| 2. Atwood | $8 Million |

# YouTube Video Marketing Overview

Promotes products and tours with other Youtubers.

3. Lilly Singh          $7.5 Million

Makes comedy skits mostly featuring herself talking about her parents and relationship issues.

| YouTube name/channel | 2016 Income |
|---|---|
| 4. Smosh | $7 Million |
| Comedy Duo. | |
| 5. Rosanna Pasino Nerdie Nummies | $6 Million |
| Baking show | |
| 6. Markipler | $5.5 Million |
| Comments on Video Games. | |
| 7. German Garmendia | $5.5 Million |
| Got a publishing deal from his YouTube channel | |
| 8. Miranda Sings | $5 Million |
| Comedian | |

# YouTube Video Marketing
# Overview

9. Collen Ballinger $5 Million

Comedian

10. Tyler Oakley $5 Million

Makes a diary. LGBT Activist


And these are just some the the top earners. There are many more making $50,000 a month talking about movies, how to put on make up or video taping a day at an amusement park.

A Few Keys to Video Marketing Success

1. Commitment

While many of the top YouTubers are funny, they take their business seriously. One of the first things you have to understand is that there is commitment needed to be successful on YouTube.

Many of the successful YouTubers put up video's daily! One such YouTuber is Grace Randolph (Beyond the Trailer). Grace comments on movie news and movie trailers. She typically uploads 3 video's a day.

# YouTube Video Marketing Overview

## 2. Research

Just putting up a video will not guarantee views. You have to put in research for every video. Research if the topic is popular or trending. Research what keywords you should use in your video. Research the success of other video's. Skip the research, skip the success.

## 3. Popularity

There are certain topics on YouTube that are extremely popular. Star Wars, Disney, Scantily clad women, video games, comedy. Know the level of your topics popularity and try to use keyword planning to max out the highest possible level. Some educational material is extremely valuable, but not popular.

## ZERO COST MARKETING OVERVIEW

This is a zero cost online  marketing plan for any business, cause or idea you wish to promote. This plan will show you step by step how to use online marketing featuring YouTube and Article Marketing to get free advertising for this or any product. In addition, this report will show you how to use this zero cost marketing plan to create a passive income stream.

# YouTube Video Marketing Overview

### A Few Key Definitions

YouTube is a video-sharing website headquartered in San Bruno, California, United States. The service was created by three former PayPal employee in February 2005. In November 2006, it was bought by Google for 1.65 Billion dollars. According to the Huffington Post, YouTube has 1 billion active users each month. Or nearly one out of every two people on the internet.

AdSense (Google AdSense) is an advertising placement service by Google. The program is designed for website publishers who want to display targeted text, video or image advertisement on website pages and earn money when the site visitors view or click the ads.

Hyperlink is a link from a hypertext file or document to another location or file, typically activated by clicking on a highlighted word or image on the screen.

### Black Hat

In search engine optimization (SEO) terminology, black hat SEO refers to the use of aggressive SEO strategies, techniques and tactics that focus only on search engines and not a human audience, and usually does not obey search engines guidelines.

# YouTube Video Marketing
## Overview

### Getting Started

You get started by opening up a YouTube account. Go to www.YouTube.com and follow the step by step instructions. Then you open up a AdSense account. The AdSense account will take about a week to open. AdSense is linked to your YouTube account and land bank account. AdSense will use your 9 digit routing number to deposit a small amount of money into your land bank account. You then have to report to AdSense the amount deposited. After the deposit is confirmed, AdSense will send you a postcard to verify your address. You must then report to AdSense the pin number locate on the postcard. Once all the verification takes place YouTube allows you to connect all of the accounts and by doing so, you can now monetize your video's and create a passive income stream.

### Social Media

You should join Social Media web sites like Facebook, Google Plus, Digg, Twitter, Linkedin, Tumbler and Pinterest. Every time you upload a video. When you are finished Optimizing it, you should link it to all of your social media web sites. This creates Backlinks. A Backlink is an incoming hyperlink from one webpage to another. Google and YouTube will rank your video higher if it has a good number of Backlinks. However if you have too many, and it appears that you have created them artificially, then Google and YouTube can punish you by removing your video.

# YouTube Video Marketing
# Overview

As long as you are backlinking organically and not using Black Hat software or Black Hat web sites, you should be find with Google and YouTube.

## Show Me the Money!

Monetization involves you allowing AdSense to place ads that run before or are placed on your videos. If the ads are clicked on, you make money. If the ads are viewed in their entirety you make money.

After you have your accounts set up, you need to gather all of the tools you will be using to create videos. You can create your videos using a standard video camera and tripod and videotape yourself. Or any other number of ways you can capture video. However for this program we are going "zero cost" so there will be no need to purchase or obtain a video camera.

## Getting Free Tools to Create Your Videos

We are going to use "Screen Capture" software. Go to http://screencast-o-matic.com/home to download a free screen capture software called Screencast-o-Matic. There are two versions. The Free version allows you to videotape up to 15 minutes of content and places a watermark on all of your recordings. The pro version makes longer recordings and has edit tools and not watermark. The pro version cost $15 and year and may be worth the investment once your business begins to make a profit.

# YouTube Video Marketing
## Overview

Then next tool you will use in creating your videos is a free copy of the office software package called Apache OpenOffice. Go to https://www.openoffice.org/download/ to download the software.

100% Copyright Free Content

Now that you have to tools to create a video, you need content. Wikipedia is an excellent source of copyright free content, you can use to create your videos. There are many keyword phrases that you can use to find material. Later on in this book you will learn how to use the Google Ad Planner to get the best keyword phrases to use in your videos.

# YouTube Video Marketing
# SEO – The Key to Internet Riches

## Search Engine Optimization

### Analytics: Video Viewership

Through out this book I am going to discuss many YouTube analytics that factor into how your video is ranked in YouTube. Once someone clicks onto your video to view it, YouTube keeps track of how many minutes it was view. Videos that are viewed from beginning to end get ranked higher base on the belief that the content is good if the viewer keeps watching it. For this reason, it is usually a good idea to keep most your videos under five minutes. It addition, this allows you to create more videos to a related topic. It is better to have twenty 3 minute videos than one 1 hour video, because it is more likely that the 3 minute videos will be watched in their entirety. Also by creating 20 videos you now have 20 possible places for AdSense to place monetized ads and thus increase your earning potential 20 times.

### Tags, Keywords and Keyword Phrases

Tags, keywords and keyword phrases are the most important part of getting your YouTube video to rank on the first page of YouTube. There is an old saying..."If you commit murder, where do you hide the body, where nobody will find it? On the second page of Google".

# YouTube Video Marketing
## SEO – The Key to Internet Riches

Although we are working on YouTube the principle is the same. You must rank on the first page of YouTube in order for your video to get views from standard YouTube web site traffic.

Keywords are words that relate to your video. Some keywords for business are:

Business, Marketing and Start-up

Keyword Phrases for business are:

how to make money from home, internet marketing, small business grants

Tags are Keywords or Keyword Phrases that you place on your YouTube video's editing page, in order to get viewers to find your video.

Your goal is to try to rank in the top 20(land on the first page of YouTube) for every or most of the Tags in your video.

### Your Video Title

The title of your video should be a keyword phrase that you want to rank for. It should also be relevant to the content in the video. When your title, tags and description are all relevant it boosts your YouTube rankings.

# YouTube Video Marketing
# SEO – The Key to Internet Riches

## Video Description

Each video is allowed to have a description. At the top of the description box, is where you should place a clickable or hyperlink, to either your web site or another video that you wish to viewer to see. Below the link should be a description of the video that contains content that is relative to the video. One short cut you can use it to cut and paste your video script into the description.

You video description should also have the keywords you used as tags. This adds to the videos relevancy.

You should also put links in you video to your social media addresses.

## Half Time Adjustments

Any tags that are ranking your video in the top 20 should be placed in the headline/title of the video to boost their rank even higher.

One software that helps save you a tremendous amount of time doing this is called Tube Buddy.

https://www.tubebuddy.com/

# YouTube Video Marketing
## Writing Your Script

## CREATING CONTENT

You have two options for creating content. On screen video of yourself using a digital camera or phone camera. Take notes of what you will discuss.

Know your topic before you hit record.

Recording Tips:

* Use good lighting.

* Try recording near a window during the day time.

* Limit background noise as much as possible.

* Use a POWERPOINT screen capture style video.

* Create bullet points

* Use free software like jing or camstudio to record it. You can also get a free 30 day trial of camtasia from TechSmith

* www.screencast-o-matic.com is another free solution.

* Use your computer's built in microphone.

# YouTube Video Marketing
# Writing Your Script

* Use a usb microphone is ideal, but not required.

* if you or kids have a usb gaming headset that works as well.

* most smart phones have a mp3 recording option.

## Writing Your Script

Try to use words in your script that get and hold your viewers attention. Words like... you, want, now, free, limited time, All-American, imagine and how to, are just a few of the many words that are proven to stir a viewers emotions. Viewing a few copy writing videos on YouTube should help you to chose attention grabbing words.

AIDA is an acronym used in marketing and advertising that describes a common list of events that may occur when a consumer engages with an advertisement.

- A – attention (awareness): attract the attention of the customer.
- I – interest of the customer.
- D – desire: convince customers that they want and desire the product or service and that it will satisfy their needs.
- A – action: lead customers towards taking action and/or purchasing.

# YouTube Video Marketing
## Writing Your Script

Using a system like this gives one a general understanding of how to target a market effectively. Moving from step to step, one loses some percent of prospects.

AIDA is a historical model, rather than representing current thinking in the methods of advertising effectiveness.

A basic rule of thumb for writing your script is that one paragraph equals about 60 seconds of talking. So if you are trying to shoot a 3 minute video you what to create a 3 paragraph document for your script. Try to use words in our script that are relevant to the title of your video.

You can also cut and paste your script into a YouTube video editor, and make your video Closed Captioned. This will increase your rankings in the YouTube search engine and it will allow more people to understand your video and increase your views.

## CREATING TOPICS FOR YOUR VIDEOS

It is time to brainstorm and write down topics for your videos.

Remember you could choose a video around your own information product if you had it.

# YouTube Video Marketing
## Writing Your Script

Get a notepad and think of 10 to 20 FAQ about your business.

http://answers.yahoo.com

Is a good source to find out what the potiential customers of your business are interested in.

Also look at articles on ezinearticles.com and see what topics come up the most for articles related to your business.

You can also browse forums related to your business.

Take a look at information products about your target market.

When you make a video that features Frequently Asked Questions each faq could be a short 1 to 3 minute video.

Use nichesuggest.com for a list of possible keyword ideas as well as seocentro and the google keyword planner.

Brainstorm 5 to 10 additional solution oriented videos. You should cover why the solution you are offering is better and why does your product recommendation solve your customer's problem.

# YouTube Video Marketing
## Writing Your Script

Try to think of every advantage possible. Read other reviews of similar products or businesses or view sales pages for ideas of content for your videos.

### Creating a Multipurpose Close

There are certain things that you should say in almost all of your videos:

* Thank the viewer for watching

* Ask the viewer to Thumbs up or Like your video

* Ask the viewer to subscribe to your YouTube Channel

* Ask the viewer to leave a comment

* Ask the viewer to share your video link with friends or social media

# YouTube Video Marketing
# Writing Your Script

### YOUR CALL TO ACTION

send your website visitors to a variety of places.

* A free website through weebly.com

* A free page through squidoo.com

*  A free blog through blogspot.com

Use a tracking link like www.bit.ly or www.tinyurl.com

be careful as these links can change on you.

# YouTube Video Marketing
## Writing Your Script

## UPLOADING VIDEO

Create your account at www.youtube.com you can use a google account if you have one already created. Upload your video. Then provide your keyword rich video title. Look at other examples of videos performing well in that space. Use keywords from your niche or business and topic research write a good description with the keywords in it.

Try to include at least 2 sentences in your description. More content in your description will not hurt you. Include your website link at the beginning of the description use format http://www.yourfreelink.com encourage likes, comments, or honest feedback at the end of the description. Make a call to action in the description as well.

# Chapter 8

# Millionaire
# Real Estate
# Rolodex

**Get Started Fast with these Business Web Sites**

# MILLIONAIRE ROLODEX

As of the writing of this book, all of the companies web site's are up and running. From time to time companies go out of business or change their web address.  So, instead of just giving you just 1 source I give you plenty of sources to choose from.

## Top 15 Most Popular eBizMBA Rank

## Real Estate Websites

### with Estimated Unique Monthly Visitors

1. **Zillow**                36,000,000

2. **Trulia**                23,000,000

3. **Yahoo! Homes**          20,000,000

4. **Realtor**               18,000,000

5. **Redfin**                6,000,000

6. **Homes**                 5,000,000

# MILLIONAIRE ROLODEX

## Top 15 Most Popular eBizMBA Rank

| Real Estate Websites | Monthly Visitors |
| --- | --- |
| 7. ApartmentGuide | 2,500,000 |
| 8. Curbed | 2,000,000 |
| 9. ReMax | 1,800,000 |
| 10. HotPads | 1,750,000 |
| 11. ZipRealty | 1,600,000 |
| 12. Apartments | 1,500,000 |
| 13. Rent | 1,400,000 |
| 14. Auction | 1,300,000 |
| 15. ForRent | 1,200,000 |

# MILLIONAIRE ROLODEX

## Nationwide Banks & Foreclosure Properties

## Bank of America

http://foreclosures.bankofamerica.com/

## Wells Fargo

https://reo.wellsfargo.com/

## Ocwen Financial Corporation

http://www.ocwen.com/reo

## Hubzu

http://www.hubzu.com/

# MILLIONAIRE ROLODEX

## Government Foreclosure Properties

### Fannie Mae
### The Federal National Mortgage Association

https://www.fanniemae.com/singlefamily/reo-vendors

### Department of Housing and Urban Development

https://www.hudhomestore.com/Home/Index.aspx

### The Federal Deposit Insurance Corporation

https://www.fdic.gov/buying/owned/

### The United States Department of Agriculture

https://properties.sc.egov.usda.gov/resales/index.jsp

### United States Marshals

https://www.usmarshals.gov/assets/sales.htm#real_estate

# MILLIONAIRE ROLODEX

## Commercial Real Estate Properties

## City Feet

http://www.cityfeet.com/#

## The Commercial Real Estate Listing Service

https://www.cimls.com/

## Land . Net

http://www.land.net/

## Loop . Net

http://www.loopnet.com/

# MILLIONAIRE ROLODEX

## FSBO – For Sale By Owner Properties

### By Owner

http://www.byowner.com/

### For sale by owner in Canada

http://www.fsbo-bc.com/

### For sale by owner Central

http://www.fsbocentral.com/

### For sale by Owner: world's largest FSBO web site

http://www.forsalebyowner.com/

### Ranch by owner

http://www.ranchbyowner.com/

# MILLIONAIRE ROLODEX

## Tools to Get You Started Video Marketing

https://www.YouTube.com/

Upload your videos to this web site.


https://www.wikipedia.org/

Get valuable information for video topics.


https://screencast-o-matic.com/

Use this screen capture software to create videos


http://www.openoffice.org/download/

Use this Open source word processor software to make slides for your videos.

# MILLIONAIRE ROLODEX

## Free Keyword Tools

## Google keyword planner

https://adwords.google.com/home/tools/keyword-planner/

## SEO Centro

http://www.seocentro.com/

## Ubersuggest

https://ubersuggest.io/

## Promoting Your Real Estate/Videos

## Top Free Press Release Websites

https://www.prlog.org

https://www.pr.com

https://www.pr-inside.com

https://www.newswire.com

https://www.OnlinePRNews.com

# MILLIONAIRE ROLODEX

## Top Social Media Websites

https://www.facebook.com

https://www.tumbler.com

https://www.pinterest.com

https://www.reddit.com

https://www.linkedin.com/

http://digg.com/

https://twitter.com

https://instagram.com

## For Everything Under the Sun at Wholesale Prices

**http://www.liquidation.com/**

## COMPUTERS/Office Equipment

**http://www.wtsmedia.com/**

**http://www.laptopplaza.com/**

**http://www.outletpc.com/**

# MILLIONAIRE ROLODEX

With this "Millionaire Rolodex" of real estate business resources, you have a ton of web sites that you can use to get started working on your real estate business with little to no money.

So take advantage of these resources to continue to gain valuable knowledge, save money and promote your real estate business.

# Chapter 9

# REAL ESTATE
# Terms

# Real Estate Terms

**Acceleration Clause** - A contract provision that allows a lender to require a borrower to repay all or part of an outstanding loan if certain requirements are not met. An acceleration clause outlines the reasons that the lender can demand loan repayment. Also known as "acceleration covenant".

**Active Income** - Active income is income for which services have been performed. This includes wages, tips, salaries, commissions and income from businesses in which there is material participation.

**Agent** - One who is legally authorized to act on behalf of another person.

**All-inclusive deed of trust (AITD)** - An All Inclusive Trust Deed (AITD) is a new deed of trust that includes the balance due on the existing note plus new funds advanced; also known as a wrap-around mortgage.

**Amortized loan** - An amortized loan is a loan with scheduled periodic payments that consist of both principal and interest. An amortized loan payment pays the relevant interest expense for the period before any principal is paid and reduced.

# Real Estate Terms

**Appraiser** - A practitioner who has the knowledge and expertise necessary to estimate the value of an asset, or the likelihood of an event occurring, and the cost of such an occurrence.

**Asking price** - the price at which something is offered for sale.

**Assignment** - An assignment (Latin cessio) is a term used with similar meanings in the law of contracts and in the law of real estate. In both instances, it encompasses the transfer of rights held by one party—the assignor—to another party—the assignee.

**At-risk rule** - Tax laws limiting the amount of losses an investor (usually a limited partner) can claim. Only the amount actually at risk can be deducted.

**Balloon mortgage -** a mortgage in which a large portion of the borrowed principal is repaid in a single payment at the end of the loan period.

**Capital gain** - a profit from the sale of property or of an investment.

**Cash flow** - the total amount of money being transferred into and out of a business, especially as affecting liquidity.

# Real Estate Terms

**Chattel** - an item of property other than real estate.

**Co-insurance** - a type of insurance in which the insured pays a share of the payment made against a claim.

**Contract of sale** - A real estate contract is a contract between parties for the purchase and sale, exchange, or other conveyance of real estate.

**Declining balance method** - A declining balance method is a common depreciation-calculation system that involves applying the depreciation rate against the non-depreciated balance.

**Depreciation** - Depreciation is an accounting method of allocating the cost of a tangible asset over its useful life. Businesses depreciate long-term assets for both tax and accounting purposes.

**Earnest money** - Earnest money is a deposit made to a seller showing the buyer's good faith in a transaction. Often used in real estate transactions, earnest money allows the buyer additional time when seeking financing. Earnest money is typically held jointly by the seller and buyer in a trust or escrow account.

# Real Estate Terms

**Equity participation** - Equity participation is the ownership of shares in a company or property. ... The greater the equity participation rate, the higher the percentage of shares owned by stakeholders. Allowing stakeholders to own shares ties the stakeholders' success with that of the company or real estate investment.

**Estoppel** - Estoppel Certificate. An estoppel certificate is a document used in mortgage negotiations to establish facts and financial obligations, such as outstanding amounts due that can affect the settlement of a loan. It is required by a lender of a third party in a real estate transaction.

**Fee simple** - In English law, a fee simple or fee simple absolute is an estate in land, a form of freehold ownership. It is a way that real estate may be owned in common law countries, and is the highest possible ownership interest that can be held in real property.

**Gift deed** - Quitclaim Deed Vs. Gift Deed. Property deeds define and protect ownership in a home. In real estate, deeds are legal documents that transfer ownership of a property from one party to another. ... Each type of deed is used for a specific situation.

# Real Estate Terms

**Gross income** - A real estate investment term, Gross Operating Income refers to the result of subtracting the credit and vacancy losses from a property's gross potential income. Also Known As: Effective Gross Income (EGI)

**Income approach to value** - The income approach is a real estate appraisal method that allows investors to estimate the value of a property by taking the net operating income of the rent collected and dividing it by the capitalization rate.

**Interest** - Estates and ownership interests defined. The law recognizes different sorts of interests, called estates, in real property. The type of estate is generally determined by the language of the deed, lease, bill of sale, will, land grant, etc., through which the estate was acquired.

**Joint and several note** - Joint and several note is a promissory note which is the note of all and of each of the makers as to its legal obligation between the parties to it.

# Real Estate Terms

**Lease option** - A lease option (more formally Lease With the Option to Purchase) is a type of contract used in both residential and commercial real estate. In a lease-option, a property owner and tenant agree that, at the end of a specified rental period for a given property, the renter has the option of purchasing the property.

**Like kind property** - Like-Kind Property. Any two assets or properties that are considered to be the same type, making an exchange between them tax free. To qualify as like kind, two assets must be of the same type (e.g. two pieces of residential real estate), but do not have to be of the same quality.

**Loan to value** - The loan to value or LTV ratio of a property is the percentage of the property's value that is mortgaged. ... Loan to Value is used in commercial real estate as well. Examples: $300,000 appraised value of a home. $240,000 mortgage on the property. $240,000 / $300,000 = .80 or 80% Loan to Value Ratio

**Mortgage broker** - A mortgage broker is an intermediary working with a borrower and a lender while qualifying the borrower for a mortgage. The broker gathers income, asset and employment documentation, a credit report and other information for assessing the borrower's ability to secure financing.

# Real Estate Terms

**Net rentable area** - Actual square-unit of a building that may be leased or rented to tenants, the area upon which the lease or rental payments are computed. It usually excludes common areas, elevator shafts, stairways, and space devoted to cooling, heating, or other equipment. Also called net leasable area.

**Option** - A real estate purchase option is a contract on a specific piece of real estate that allows the buyer the exclusive right to purchase the property. Once a buyer has an option to buy a property, the seller cannot sell the property to anyone else.

**Possession** - A principle of real estate law that allows a person who possesses someone else's land for an extended period of time to claim legal title to that land.

**Prepayment penalty** - Prepayment Penalty. A prepayment penalty is a clause in a mortgage contract stating that a penalty will be assessed if the mortgage is prepaid within a certain time period. The penalty is based on a percentage of the remaining mortgage balance or a certain number of months' worth of interest.

# Real Estate Terms

**Promissory note** - In the United States, a mortgage note (also known as a real estate lien note, borrower's note) is a promissory note secured by a specified mortgage loan; it is a written promise to repay a specified sum of money plus interest at a specified rate and length of time to fulfill the promise.

**Real estate owned (REO)** - Real estate owned or REO is a term used in the United States to describe a class of property owned by a lender—typically a bank, government agency, or government loan insurer—after an unsuccessful sale at a foreclosure auction.

**Refinancing** - Getting a new mortgage to replace the original is called refinancing. Refinancing is done to allow a borrower to obtain a better interest term and rate. The first loan is paid off, allowing the second loan to be created, instead of simply making a new mortgage and throwing out the original mortgage.

**Reproduction cost** - The costs involved with identically reproducing an asset or property with the same materials and specifications as an insured property based on current prices.

# Real Estate Terms

**Right of survivorship** - The right of survivorship is an attribute of several types of joint ownership of property, most notably joint tenancy and tenancy in common. When jointly owned property includes a right of survivorship, the surviving owner automatically absorbs a dying owner's share of the property. Thus if A and B jointly own a house with a right of survivorship, and B dies, A becomes the sole owner of the house, despite any contrary intent in B's will.

**Standby commitment** - A standby commitment is a formal agreement by a bank agreeing to lend money to a borrower up to a specified amount for a specific period. It is also known as firm commitment lending. The amount given under standby commitment is to be used only in specified contingency.

**Supply and demand** - The law of supply and demand is a basic economic principle that explains the relationship between supply and demand for a good or service and how the interaction affects the price of that good or service. The relationship of supply and demand affects the housing market and the price of a house

# Real Estate Terms

**Tenancy by entirety** - Tenants by entirety (TBE) is a method in some states by which married couples can hold the title to a property. In order for one spouse to modify his or her interest in the property in any way, the consent of both spouses is required by tenants by entirety.

**Title insurance policy** - Title insurance is an insurance policy that covers the loss of ownership interest in a property due to legal defects and is required if the property is under mortgage. The most common type of title insurance is a lender's title insurance, which is paid for by the borrower but protects only the lender.

**Vacancy and rent loss** - Vacancy and Credit Loss in real estate investing is the amount of money or percentage of net operating income that is estimated to not be realized due to non-payment of rents and vacant units

**Will** - A will or testament is a legal document by which a person, the testator, expresses their wishes as to how their property is to be distributed at death, and names one or more persons, the executor, to manage the estate until its final distribution.

# $10,000

# Massive Money Internet Marketing &

# Copy Writing & SEO Course &

# $1,000 Value Bonus

# Internet Marketing Videos

**LIBRARY I (Video Training Programs)**

1. Product Creation

2. Copy Writing & Payment

3. Auto Responder & Product Download Page

4. How to start a Freelancing business

5. Video Marketing

6. List Building

7. Affiliate Marketing

8. How to Get Massive Web Site Traffic


**LIBRARY II (Video Training Programs)**

1. Goldmine Government Grants

2. How to Write a Business Plan

3. Secrets to making money on eBay

4. Credit Repair

5. Goal Setting

6. Asset Protection How to Incorporate

# $10,000 MegaSized Internet Marketing &

# Copy Writing & SEO Course &

# $1,000 Value Bonus

Library III

**1. SEO SIMPLIFIED PART 1**

**2. SEO SIMPLIFIED PART 2**

**3. SEO Private Network Blogs**

**4. SEO Social Signals**

**5. SEO Profits**

Bonus 1000 Package!

**1. Insider Secrets to Government Contracts (PDF)**

**2. 1000 Books/Guides (text files)**

**3. Vacation Discounts (text file w/links to discounts)**

**4. Media Players (3 Software Programs)**

**100% MONEY BACK GUARANTEE!!!**

**ALL ON A 8 GIGABYTE FLASH DRIVE**

**This Massive Library with a $10,000 value all for only a**

## 1 time payment of $67!!!

**Get Instant Access by Using the Link Below:**

# https://urlzs.com/p7v3T

# Leave a review and join Our VIP Mailing List Then Get All our Audio Books Free! We will be releasing over 100 money making audio books within the next 12 months! Just leave a review and join our mailing list and get them all for free!

Just Hit/Type in the Link Below

https://urlzs.com/HfbGF

www.ingramcontent.com/pod-product-compliance
Lightning Source LLC
Chambersburg PA
CBHW071433210326
41597CB00020B/3779